IMAGES
of Rail

HARTFORD
COUNTY TROLLEYS

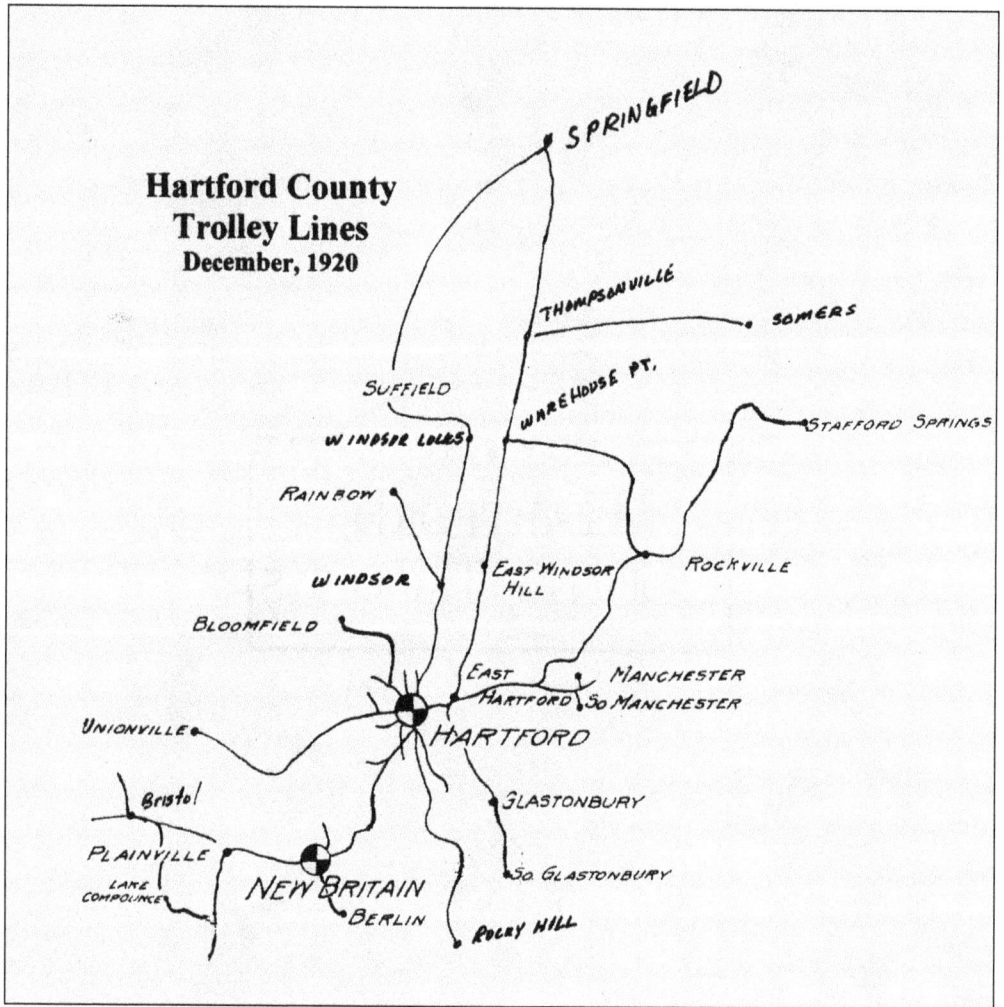

Hartford County Trolley Lines
December, 1920

SPRINGFIELD

THOMPSONVILLE   SOMERS

SUFFIELD   WAREHOUSE PT.

WINDSOR LOCKS   STAFFORD SPRINGS

RAINBOW

WINDSOR   EAST WINDSOR HILL   ROCKVILLE

BLOOMFIELD

UNIONVILLE   EAST HARTFORD   MANCHESTER
HARTFORD   So MANCHESTER

Bristol   GLASTONBURY

PLAINVILLE   So. GLASTONBURY
LAKE COMPOUNCE   NEW BRITAIN
BERLIN   ROCKY HILL

This *c.* 1920 map of streetcar lines in Hartford County reveals approximately 200 miles of track.

IMAGES
of Rail

HARTFORD
COUNTY TROLLEYS

Connecticut Trolley Museum

ARCADIA
PUBLISHING

Published by Arcadia Publishing
Charleston, South Carolina

Library of Congress Catalog Card Number: 2005931729

For all general information contact Arcadia Publishing at:
Telephone 843-853-2070
Fax 843-853-0044
E-mail sales@arcadiapublishing.com
For customer service and orders:
Toll-Free 1-888-313-2665

Visit us on the Internet at www.arcadiapublishing.com

Track work on Trinity Street is shown in this 1898 view, with the state capitol in the background. The capitol, opened in 1880, was built on the site formerly occupied by Trinity College. The Gothic building was designed by architect Richard Upjohn and cost the enormous sum of $3 million.

CONTENTS

Acknowledgments   6

Introduction   7

1.   The Bristol Line   9

2.   The Farmington Street Railway   37

3.   Downtown Hartford   41

4.   The Hartford Suburban Lines   77

5.   New Britain, Plainville, and Southington   101

6.   The Hartford and Springfield Street Railway   107

7.   The Connecticut Trolley Museum in 2005   119

ACKNOWLEDGMENTS

Many of the photographs in this book were gleaned from the Connecticut Motor Coach Museum's Horace Bromley Collection and the Connecticut Electric Railway Association Archives. Valuable assistance was rendered by Fred S. Bennett of Granby, who provided much information and gave the authors access to his extensive collection of Connecticut streetcar photographs. We would also like to thank Steve Kellner of Malden, Massachusetts, who provided material from his collection of New England transit memorabilia, and Bob Montgomery of the Bristol Historical Society, who assisted in the identification of many of the Bristol photographs. To them, we express our grateful appreciation.

—Louis Grimaldi, President
Connecticut Electric Railway Association
East Windsor, Connecticut
860-627-6540

—Alan J. Walker, President
Connecticut Motor Coach Museum
East Windsor, Connecticut
860-623-4732

Consolidated Railway car No. 486 was the first streetcar to cross the newly opened Buckley Bridge, on November 27, 1907. Streetcars would continue to use this bridge until all service east of the river was discontinued in November 1939. In 1915, the car was renumbered 933 due to a company-wide project. It ran in Hartford until being scrapped in 1937.

INTRODUCTION

Prior to 1863, people who lived in Hartford County walked to wherever they wanted to go—unless they were wealthy enough to own a horse or carriage. The largest cities in the area did not have any public transportation within their limits. Outside the cities, most people lived on farms and at least had a horse or donkey if they wished to travel anywhere. Inside the city, people lived within walking distance of their jobs. Transportation to outlying towns was available on a very limited basis, usually by hired coach or stage coach.

All that changed in 1863, when the Hartford and Wethersfield Horse Railroad started operation on a line built from the statehouse in Hartford to the Wethersfield Green. With this success, horsecar lines gradually spread out through the city and, eventually, across the river to East Hartford. The first electric streetcar ran in Hartford in 1888. In 1893, the Hartford and Wethersfield Horse Railroad became the Hartford Street Railway. By 1894, all the lines on the system were electrified. Other, smaller companies also began operating streetcar lines between smaller outlying communities such as the Hartford, Manchester and Rockville Tramway.

The New Britain Tramway introduced travel by horsecars to New Britain in the late 1880s. Since transportation by horsecar was well received, the lines expanded and the system was electrified by 1893. In 1901, Connecticut Railway and Lighting became the operating company of the lines that radiated out of New Britain.

In 1905, the Consolidated Railway, a subsidiary of the New Haven Railroad, purchased the Hartford Street Railway and the Hartford, Manchester and Rockville Tramway. In 1906, the Consolidated Railway leased the Connecticut Railway and Lighting Company, which operated the lines in the New Britain area, for 99 years. In 1907, the Consolidated Railway merged with the New Haven Railroad. During a financial restructuring in 1910, the New Haven Railroad transferred all its street railway properties, both owned and leased, to a new operator: the Connecticut Company.

By 1910, three operating companies provided all the service in Hartford County: Bristol Traction, the Connecticut Company, and the Hartford and Springfield Street Railway. During its peak, Hartford County had over 200 miles of tracks, both city and suburban. The Hartford division of the Connecticut Company accounted for 145 miles—by far the major provider of public transportation in central Connecticut. The Hartford and Springfield Street Railway was the next largest provider with 47 miles, followed by the Bristol Traction Company with only 13 miles.

The peak year for the street railway industry in North America was 1914, when over 14 billion riders were carried. Afterward, the industry began a decline from which it never recovered. The abandonment of rail lines and the conversion of routes to motor coach service started in 1921.

It is interesting to note that the Southington and Plantsville Tramway was totally abandoned in 1898, well prior to the decline of streetcar usage in the state. The line was built in 1896 and only operated for two years before the property and all the equipment was auctioned off, resulting in a lack of streetcar service to this area for many years. Later, the Connecticut Company actually replaced the track on this line and provided service between New Britain and New Haven.

In addition to the Connecticut Company lines, the New Haven Railroad also operated electric lines under its own name. Two of these lines were from Hartford to Bristol and a branch from New Britain to Berlin. These two lines operated from 1898 until 1908, using what was referred to

7

as a "third rail" system for power. A third rail, which provided electrical power for the streetcar, was placed between the two rails on which the wheels of the car ran, in the center of the track. This proved to be somewhat of a safety hazard.

Since the New Haven Railroad did not have its own streetcars, some of the passenger equipment used on these lines consisted of streetcars from other companies that had been modified to railroad standards. These included four former Hartford Street Railway 15-bench open cars. The New Haven called them "open motors." Similar equipment was used in Massachusetts on the Nantasket Beach line outside Boston. Some of the Nantasket Beach cars also operated in Connecticut.

The Hartford and Springfield Street Railway had vanished by 1926, and today many of the areas it served in East Windsor, Enfield, Somers, and Suffield are still without public transportation. The Bristol Traction Company converted its lines to motor coach in 1935, and the entire Hartford division of the Connecticut Company followed suit, running exclusively motor coaches on its lines by July 1941.

The New Haven Railroad continued to operate the Connecticut Company bus lines until 1963, when it was sold to E. Clayton Gengras, a Hartford businessman. Gengras upgraded the service with new equipment and improved schedules. In the late 1960s, the Connecticut Company experimented with a city bus modified to run either on the highway or on rails. Existing rail lines to Manchester and Bloomfield were selected for the experiment; however, technical problems with the equipment and the amount of staffing required by labor contracts with the rail unions caused the cancellation of the project. One of the prototype city buses has been preserved and can be found at the Connecticut Trolley Museum in East Windsor.

The Connecticut Company bus operation was purchased by the state of Connecticut in 1976 and operates today as Connecticut Transit. Many of the bus routes still follow the paths of former streetcar lines. Only one three-mile portion of the original 200 miles of track in Hartford County remains today, now in use by the Connecticut Trolley Museum in East Windsor.

Single-truck closed car No. 16 runs on the East Main Street line in New Britain with an unidentified crew in 1910. (Steve Kellner Collection.)

One

THE BRISTOL LINE

Shown here in 1898, the Bristol railroad station was part of the New Haven Railroad system. The open car sitting at the platform was a former Hartford Street Railway open car purchased by the New Haven Railroad for the suburban service between Hartford and Bristol. The line to Bristol was electrified with a center-running third rail in 1898 to supply 600 volts DC to the cars. Local opposition to the dangers of the unprotected third rail was the primary reason the system was shut down and replaced by steam trains in 1908.

Bristol Traction Company car No. 45 runs near the Plainville switch on November 25, 1934. Within a year, the Bristol Traction Company would be an all motor coach operation. In 1965, the company would be sold to the New Britain Transportation Company.

The Bristol and Plainville Tramway Company, organized in 1893, decorated its cars in the tradition of the steam railroads with gold leaf and elegant lettering. The company was renamed Bristol Traction in 1927.

This photograph offers a view of the original Bristol and Plainville Tramway Company carbarn, located on Riverside Avenue. The Bristol and Plainville Tramway Company was chartered and organized on June 14, 1893. During its operating lifetime, it was also called the Bristol and Plainville Electric Company and finally, in 1927, the Bristol Traction Company, operating under that name until New Britain Transportation Company purchased it in 1965.

Snow removal was a concern for streetcar companies during the winter months. They had plows such as the little, single-truck Bristol Traction Company plow No. 2 in 1935. This little unit was the workhorse of the line's snow-removal operations. All summer long, it would sit in the Riverside Avenue carbarn just waiting for the temperature to drop and the snow to fall after Thanksgiving Day.

This single-truck open car was one of the original Bristol and Plainville Tramway Company cars, shown here about 1900. Bristol's population in 1900 was 9,684; by 1920, it had grown to over 20,000—no doubt helped by the fine city transit system. Bristol was known for its manufacture of clocks, ball bearings, watches, and all types of brass goods.

Before the days of air-conditioning, people took rides on open cars just to cool off. From the spring to the fall, the open car was the choice of the riding public. Between 1921 and 1927, the company operated under the Bristol and Plainville Electric name. In the 1922 company report to the Public Utilities Commission, streetcar revenue of $164,485, gas $206,651, and electric $587,589—all profits from gas and electric distribution—were credited back to the street railway portion of the business, which explains why Bristol had streetcar service in the 1920s, well after cities of similar size had lost theirs.

The streetcars and railroad trains used separate trackage, as shown in this 1918 photograph of the railroad bridge on Main Street above, with the single-truck open car below.

Open car No. 22 lays over between runs in front of the Bristol Post Office in August 1930.

Lake Compounce Park was built long before streetcar service was available in Bristol. The first cars arrived at Lake Compounce Park on August 13, 1895. The Bristol system was isolated from the rest of the vast streetcar system in Connecticut. The Connecticut Company also had a line to Lake Compounce, but the two routes did not connect.

Late in their lives, many passenger cars were converted to work cars. This former open car converted to a work car is shown at the Bristol carbarn in 1933.

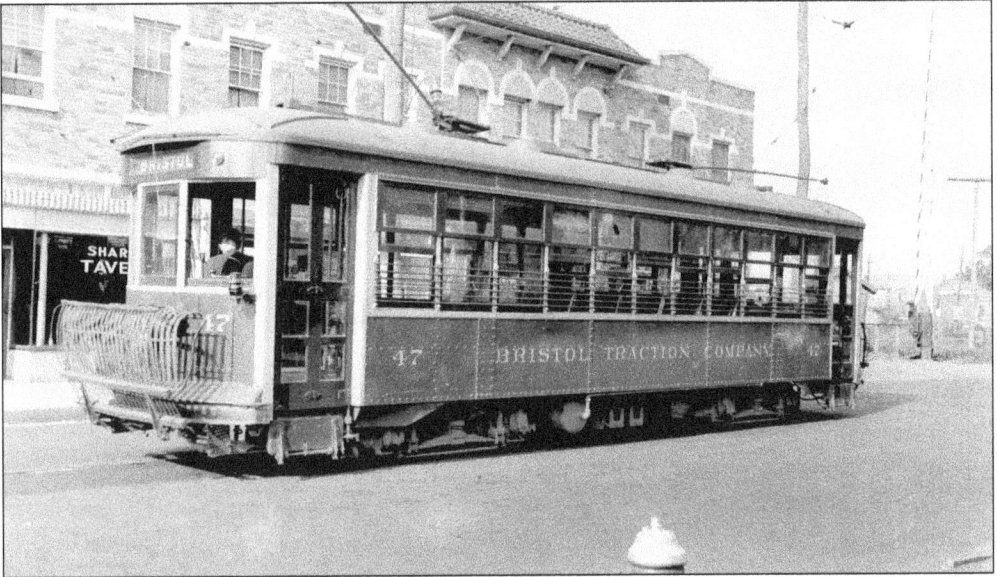

Car No. 47 sits at the end of the line in Plainville about 1934. Passengers crossed the New Haven Railroad tracks to board cars for New Britain or New Haven.

Bristol streetcar passengers traveled in style even in the last year of streetcar operation. In this 1935 view on Riverside Avenue near Main Street, car Nos. 42 and 44 accept passengers. Bristol Savings Bank appears in the background; this building is now inhabited by Webster Bank.

Streetcars first operated in Bristol in June 1893, using single-truck cars. By the 1930s, the fleet had been modernized with cars similar to No. 42, pictured here. Car Nos. 38 through 47, purchased from the Fitchburg and Leominster Street Railway in Massachusetts, were the last streetcars purchased by the Bristol Traction Company. These cars, along with the others operating on the line, were painted orange.

Traveling on North Main Street in 1935, this car is bound for Plainville. In this, the last year of streetcar operation, the company operated 11.7 miles of track and had 20 passenger cars and two work cars on the roster.

Having finished its run, car No. 38 rests at the end of the Terryville line, waiting for its next load of passengers in May 1935.

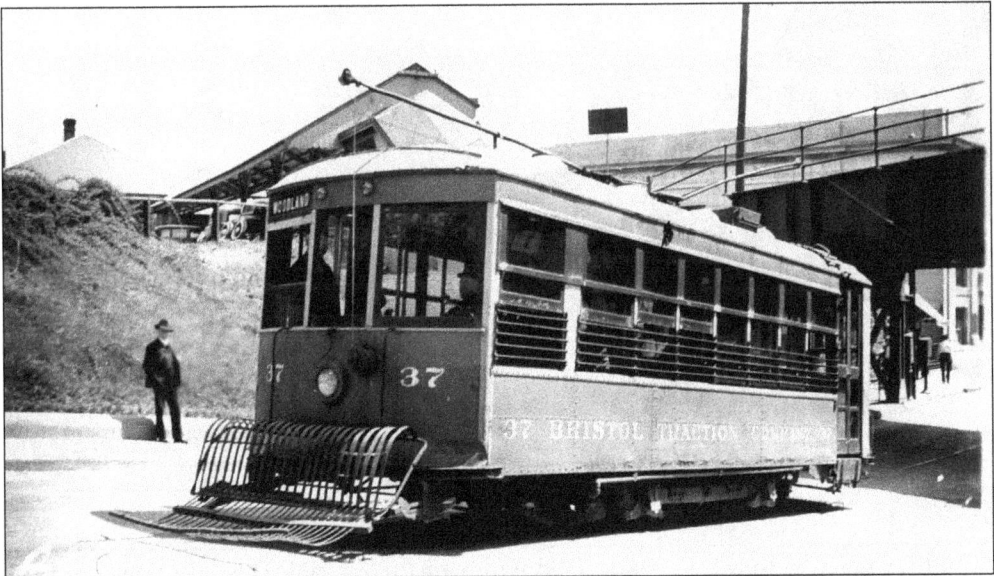

Single-truck lightweight car No. 37 runs with a load of passengers on the Woodland Street line, today crossing under New Haven Railroad's Hartford-Waterbury main line.

Car No. 37 heads north on Main Street.

Bristol Traction Company No. 26 is pictured at the carbarn rear yard. This older single-truck car was kept on the equipment list as the backup for lightweight car No. 37, which normally ran on the Woodland Street line.

The Bristol and Plainville Tramway Company was chartered and organized on June 14, 1893. By 1895, the company reported to the Public Utilities Commission 7.3 miles of track in operation with three closed and six open passenger cars. One of the closed cars is shown here on Main Street in 1900.

Two cars meet each other on the Terryville line in the 1930s. During most of its operation, the Bristol streetcar line ran on a 20-minute headway, with cars meeting at designated points, because only one track was used for both directions.

In 1935, the Forestville section of Bristol was still fairly rural, as shown in this photograph of car No. 46 at Avon Street. (Steve Kellner Collection.)

In this 1932 scene, a Bristol-bound car runs on the private right-of-way on the Plainville line. The Bristol lines were all built to a gauge of four feet eight and a half inches, like the other streetcar and railroad lines in Connecticut. Without any physical connection to the extensive Connecticut streetcar network, Bristol cars spent their entire operating life on their own network of trackage. Cars from the other operating companies such as the Connecticut Company and the Hartford and Springfield Street Railway, however, regularly ran over each other's lines.

This view depicts the Forestville section of Bristol on the Plainville line, traveled by one of the former Fitchburg and Leominster Street Railway cars.

Three cars meet at Lake Compounce Junction at one of the passing tracks in 1935. The Bristol system was a single-track operation during its entire existence, and passing tracks were located every few miles along the 12 miles of main line. The line never had the luxury of a signal system like the larger Connecticut Company; cars were operated using a timetable and verbal orders.

Two of the former Fitchburg and Leominster Railway cars meet at Lake Compounce Junction. The Lake Compounce line was typically very busy during the months when the park was open, but nearly empty during the winter months.

Bristol Traction put on a brave face amidst the growing competition from automobiles and buses in the 1930s.

22

An unidentified member of the Bristol car shop staff appears at the carbarn with two out-of-service cars in this 1900 scene. (F. S. Bennett Collection.)

This 1920s view of the Bristol railroad station shows both rail and streetcar service available at the time. The same scene, decades earlier in 1898, is on page 9. (F. S. Bennett Collection.)

Car No. 16 sits at the Terryville carbarn, waiting to depart on its next run to Bristol, in 1900. (F. S. Bennett Collection.)

Open cars, such as this one running on the Terryville line in 1898, were very popular with the riding public. Despite this, the cars had many operational disadvantages. The open sides could potentially cause accidents as riders boarded or exited, and these cars were only used May through October. During the winter months, they sat in a heated carbarn. (F. S. Bennett Collection.)

The easiest way to deliver a streetcar is on the rails under its own power, which is exactly what was done with car No. 33 in 1917. Bristol and Plainville Tramway Company car No. 33 was run under its own power from the Wason Manufacturing Company in Springfield to Bristol via the Connecticut Company to Lake Compounce. Both companies had tracks to the lake, although they did not connect. The car was then jacked up and slid over to the Bristol and Plainville Tramway Company tracks. (F. S. Bennett Collection.)

Car No. 31 appears at the Wason Manufacturing plant in Springfield prior to delivery to the Bristol and Plainville Tramway. Car Nos. 30 through 36 were all delivered via Lake Compounce, such as No. 33, shown in the previous photograph. (F. S. Bennett Collection.)

No. 34 is pictured at the Wason plant in 1917, prior to delivery to the Bristol Traction Company. The body of this car now resides at the Connecticut Trolley Museum in East Windsor. (F. S. Bennett Collection.)

A small company its entire life, the Bristol and Plainville Tramway never had the luxury of owning a car dedicated to working on the overhead wire like the much larger Connecticut Company. Here, the overhead line crew uses a snowplow as a line car, enabling work on the overhead. (F. S. Bennett Collection.)

Bristol Traction Company No. 26 sits at the end of the Woodland Street line with motorman William Harbert (left) and conductor James Thomas. This car was only used as a backup for the regular car, No. 37, when it was in the shop. Because of this, No. 26 ran until the system converted to bus in 1935. Thomas continued working for the company as a bus driver until the 1960s. (F. S. Bennett Collection.)

Track workers, mostly of Irish or Italian heritage, referred to shovels as "Irish Banjos." Sometimes the crew was able to convince the neighborhood kids to help with shoveling the snow, as in this 1920s scene on the Plainville line. (F. S. Bennett Collection.)

In the 1930s, open car No. 1 was donated to Lake Compounce for display at the park. In the above photograph, the car is loaded onto dollies at the Bristol carbarn; below, it is transported over the road to the park. (F. S. Bennett Collection.)

Sometime in the 1940s, the body of car No. 1, which had become derelict, was unceremoniously pushed into the lake, where it is reported to still sit to this day. (F. S. Bennett Collection.)

Much of the removal of snow from the tracks was done by hand. Often it meant that the entire track and carbarn crew was on snow-removal duty, as in this 1921 image of the Plainville line. (F. S. Bennett Collection.)

Often the tracks ran in the middle of the road, and snow removal meant that part of the street was shoveled also, as evidenced here in 1921 on the line to Plainville. (F. S. Bennett collection.)

30

Trolley cars did not run until the snow was completely removed from the tracks. The number of employees needed to remove this snow represented a large bite out of the budget. By the looks of it, the winter of 1921 had its share of snow. (F. S. Bennett Collection.)

With the advent of motorized motor coaches, many trolley lines were abandoned and eventually torn up. Here, open car No. 27 transports the wrecking crew while the Lake Compounce line is being torn up in the 1930s. (F. S. Bennett Collection.)

While trolley cars needed maintenance, it was not like the maintenance required by the trains of the day. The interior of the Bristol carbarn, pictured here in 1905, reflects this. (F. S. Bennett Collection.)

Barns for trolley cars did not need to be as large as those for locomotives. Often they fit right into the populated areas, as shown in this view of the carbarn in Bristol. (F. S. Bennett Collection.)

A crew tears up track on the Lake Compounce line in the 1930s. The open car offered little protection from the wind and inclement weather. (F. S. Bennett Collection.)

Early in the development of streetcars, single-truck cars such as car No. 9, shown almost brand-new in this 1898 view, were used in Bristol. Later, in the evolution of the trolley system, larger cars predominated. (F. S. Bennett Collection.)

The Bemis Car Company of Amesbury, Massachusetts, built car No. 12. Open cars were very labor intensive, as they required a two-man crew because of the open sides. The conductor collected the fares by walking on the running boards while the car was in motion. (F. S. Bennett Collection.)

In areas like Forestville Center, dirt roads were still prevalent, as seen in this photograph of a Bristol-bound car in 1898. While this road still runs through Forestville Center today, it is paved and most of the buildings in the background have been replaced with newer structures. (F. S. Bennett Collection.)

The Bristol Traction Company line ended at the railroad tracks in Plainville. Here, car No. 11 sits at the end of the line, waiting to return to Bristol, in 1898. (F. S. Bennett Collection.)

Several modes of transportation operated in Forestville Center in 1898. Trolley cars and horse and buggy are shown here. (F. S. Bennett Collection.)

Car No. 28 was sold in the 1930s to become a shed in someone's yard. In the 1960s, it was acquired and moved to the Connecticut Trolley Museum in East Windsor, where it sits today in the Northern carbarn waiting for the day when it will be restored to operation. (F. S. Bennett Collection.)

Two

THE FARMINGTON
STREET RAILWAY

Farmington Street Railway open car No. 1 appears at the end of the line in Unionville in 1907. With all the bunting on the building, this photograph was likely taken on July 4. On August 10, 1908, No. 1 was involved in a collision near Unionville with a work car. Jackie Walsh, the motorman of the work car, was killed. Both cars were repaired by the Connecticut Company Vernon Street shop in Hartford. (F. S. Bennett Collection.)

Farmington Street Railway car No. 29 was built in 1907 by the Wason Manufacturing Company of Springfield, Massachusetts. In 1910, the Farmington Street Railway was acquired by the Connecticut Company, whereupon No. 29 became No. 931.

The Unionville carbarn and shops of the Farmington Street Railway, seen here in 1908, was much different from the carbarn found in Bristol. Unionville was still much more rural than Bristol in 1908. Car No. 25 (left) had recently been delivered by the Wason Manufacturing Company.

A track gang works on the Farmington Street Railway about 1900. When trolley lines began to be built in the late 1890s, the need for laborers brought some of the first Italian families to the Hartford area. In this era, most of the track crews on the railroads and streetcar lines were either the newly arrived Italian immigrants or Irish, whose descendants first came to Connecticut in the 1820s. Most had little education and were only able to do manual labor. The arrival of the Irish and Italians brought the Roman Catholic Church to formerly Protestant Connecticut.

Although many of the trolley lines shared the road with other traffic, this streetcar bridge over the Farmington River, pictured on April 19, 1919, had a separate highway bridge. (F. S. Bennett Collection.)

The Farmington Street Railway ran from the Unionville section of Farmington to West Hartford Center. Many of the cars ended up at the Connecticut Company's Vernon Street carbarn in Hartford for heavy repairs, such as car No. 26, shown here. (F. S. Bennett Collection.)

Farmington Street Railway car No. 25 is shown in Ellington on the Hartford and Springfield Street Railway in 1914. The Farmington Street Railway was acquired by the Connecticut Company in 1910. In this scene, in which No. 25 is used as a funeral car, it still bears its Farmington Street Railway colors. In 1915, the car was repainted in Connecticut Company yellow and renumbered 1162. It ran in Hartford until 1941. The gentleman on the left is Thomas Davis, a Connecticut Company supervisor; the other two gentlemen are unidentified Hartford and Springfield Street Railway employees. (F. S. Bennett Collection.)

Three

DOWNTOWN HARTFORD

Prior to the electrification of the lines, the Hartford and Wethersfield Horse Railroad operated in Hartford with horse-drawn cars. This open horsecar, bound for Retreat Avenue, travels on Main Street in 1890.

A Hartford and Wethersfield Horse Railroad open car is shown on the Park Street line in 1890. These cars were painted lemon yellow to signify the Parkville line. Car No. 73 is only one year old in this photograph, having been built by the Newburyport Car Company of Newburyport, Massachusetts, in 1889.

This Hartford and Wethersfield Horse Railroad open car, with conductor Tom Plunket on the rear platform, was also painted yellow. Under the valance were curtains that could be unrolled in the case of inclement weather. On these cars, conductors collected fares from the running boards while the car was under way.

Two horses were used to pull this closed car on Retreat Avenue in 1893. The Retreat Avenue line cars were painted blue.

Horses were still used in 1893 on the Hartford Street Railway, as evidenced by this car traveling on State Street. By 1895, all the horsecars would be converted to electric. This car was originally green, but it was repainted in Tuscan red in 1892.

In 1889, the area at the corner of Albany Avenue and Vine Street was still considered rural and sparsely populated. The city was still confined to a small area near the Old State House. The horsecar, and later streetcar service, helped build up the area rapidly.

The Newburyport Car Company, one of the early New England builders of horse and electric streetcars, constructed car No. 2 in 1889. It is shown here at the corner of Albany Avenue and Vine Street in 1890. The company went out of business in 1905.

Car No. 10 of the Hartford and Wethersfield Horse Railroad, one of the originals built for the line, was constructed in 1863. It is pictured at Main and Asylum Streets in 1890.

This storage battery car was tested in February 1892. Battery cars carried their own power source in the form of lead acid batteries. Unfortunately, these early batteries were very primitive and undependable, so the experiment was a failure.

Shown here is a typical horsecar driver of the 1880s with his fur hat and overcoat. The cars of that era did not have enclosed front platforms for the driver or a source of heat.

Downtown Hartford bustles with pedestrian and trolley car traffic in this 1926 scene. Before World War I, an automobile was considered a luxury; by 1926, it had become a necessity, especially if one lived outside the city. (*Hartford Courant* photograph.)

The equipment shown here aids in welding together two pieces of rail in a process called thermite welding. Track men, such as those in this 1895 crew, were a tough lot, working 12 hours a day, seven days a week, and drinking hard after quitting time.

Car No. 206, built in 1894 by the J. G. Brill Company, is shown in front of the carbarn on Vernon Street in 1900. The crew prepares to take visitors to the ball game.

Hartford Street Railway car No. 211 sits at the end of the Ashley Street line in Hartford in 1900. This line was converted to motor coach operation in February 1937. This single-truck open car was built by the J. G. Brill Company of Philadelphia in 1894. It was scrapped in 1916—along with most of the single-truck open cars the Connecticut Company inherited from its predecessors.

This March 2005 view depicts Ashley Street in the same location as No. 211 above.

Motorman John Curtin (left) and conductor James Roach are pictured with open car No. 44 on Zion Street in 1910. Open cars had popular appeal at the dawn of the 20th century. They afforded not only convenient transportation but also a breeze in the warm summer months. In the early 1900s, there were over 25,000 open cars operating in the nation's cities. The major drawback to the open car from an operational standpoint was the expense of having two different sets of equipment: one for summer and one for winter.

This 2005 photograph of Zion Street was taken from the same location as that of car No. 44 in the previous view.

The new Hartford City Hall appears in this 1925 image, along with open car No. 280. The firemen are pulling one of Hartford's earliest hand-powered fire engines, called a Smith Machine. Hartford organized its fire department in 1789, one of the first in the United States. The Hartford Fire Department was completely motorized by 1922 and ranked with the best of New York or Boston. Fifteen engine companies, six hook-and-ladder companies, and one water tower protected the city in 1925.

By 1937, Hartford had grown and many new buildings had been constructed, as shown in this scene of Main Street.

Hartford was hit by a hurricane on September 21, 1938, during which the Commerce Street power station was inundated by the flooding Connecticut River. As a result, limited power was available for streetcars. Only the 1700-series cars were operated, as pictured here. These cars had just two motors and used less current than the others, which had four motors. Investment in equipment and operating logistics for a street railway in a city like Hartford was an enormous undertaking.

This 2004 view of Main Street in Hartford was taken at the corner of Main and Asylum Streets.

The traffic tower at the junction of Main Street and Albany Avenue, locally known as "the Tunnel" because the main line of the New Haven Railroad ran under the intersection, is shown here. The view looks north up Main Street. Amtrak passenger trains still run in this tunnel.

The same scene is depicted in March 2005. The traffic tower has been replaced with overhead stoplights. Just a few weeks before this photograph was taken, the city tore down the Firestone building, which had remained empty for many years and had become an eyesore.

This car, bound for Wethersfield, travels on Wethersfield Avenue past Colts Park in 1940.

This Consolidated Railway open car runs on the Farmington Avenue line at Union Station in 1907.

Traffic at the intersection of Park and Main Streets in Hartford was regulated by a police officer in 1940. Here, a trolley car travels on the K line, which ran from Park Road in West Hartford via Park, Main, and Capen Streets to the end of the line on Barbour Street.

In this 2005 image of the same location, many of the buildings no longer stand.

The motorman on the left is James Dalton; the conductor is unidentified. Prior to 1914, the hiring process for operating personal at the Connecticut Company was very informal by today's standards. After a brief interview with the chief motorman, a new employee was assigned to a motorman or conductor for training, depending on the job for which he was hired. After a 10-day training period on the various types of cars and the 21 different lines on the Hartford division, he was ready to work on a regular run.

Single-truck car No. 808 runs on the Asylum Avenue line on State Street in 1919. The early single-truck cars were fashioned closely after horsecars, still retaining the curved sides that prevented hitting the wheels of wagons in the crowded, often narrow city streets.

The Vernon Street carbarn is under construction in this 1896 photograph. Note the horse-drawn tower wagon for working on the overhead wire. This building was razed in 1990 after a new bus garage was opened in the North Meadows. Originally built to house streetcars, it was used as a bus garage and repair shop after streetcars were discontinued in 1941.

The Vernon Street carbarn is pictured in 1936. The office building in the front was razed in 1940, when a newer building was erected on the same site.

Car No. 647, along with operator Alto Anderson, sits at the end of the Cedar Hill line on Fairfield Avenue in Hartford.

Car No. 304 prepares to depart downtown Hartford for New Britain. With open cars, it was not unusual to see riders on the running boards. This car was built in 1899 by the J. G. Brill Company of Philadelphia. It became No. 419 after the 1915 passenger car renumbering.

Car No. 1801 crosses the Valley line of the New Haven Railroad on Hartford Avenue, heading toward Wethersfield, in this 1940 scene.

The warmth of the trolley car was a welcome relief from the cold. Bound for Manchester, this car accepts passengers on Market Street in winter 1936. The Travelers building and the WTIC radio tower appear in the background.

Double track is shown at Main and Tower Avenue in this scene. The conductor is identified as Fratquer (left) and the motorman as Gallipole. The car will cross over to the other track and run to Wethersfield via the Old State House.

Although the trolley tracks are gone and many new buildings have been built, the house shown in the 1914 scene above is still standing in March 2005.

A single-truck Birney car, with operator Larry Hallisey, runs on the Asylum Avenue line. These cars were designed by Charles Birney of Stone and Webster Engineering to help street railways reduce operating costs. They were inexpensive to operate and ideally suited to lines with light ridership. They were never popular with the public, however, because of the poor ride they gave. In 1924, the Asylum Avenue line became one of the first converted to motor coach in Hartford.

A Hartford, Manchester and Rockville Tramway car is bound for Rockville, while Hartford Street Railway open car No. 249 takes on passengers at the Old State House in Hartford in 1905.

Due to their urban location, streetcar lines were ideally suited for inner-city freight delivery. In this 1920 scene, Connecticut Company car No. 2018 is shown at the State Street car house with a load of express. These cars traveled all over the Connecticut Company system, delivering packages to customers, just like UPS and FedEx do today.

Middletown-bound car No. 521 travels on Franklin Avenue at Jordan Lane in 1914. After the mid-1920s, the automobile came into common use and sent the streetcar industry into a serious decline. The automobile—not the bus—was the primary threat to the streetcar. It was more convenient. The Middletown line ran for less than 25 years, only operating from 1909 to 1930, when it was cut back to Rocky Hill.

Open car No. 209, a product of the J. G. Brill Company, runs along Vine Street, bound for Hartford City Hall. Notice the split-rail fence in front of the car; this area was still farmland in 1894. The J. G. Brill Company was a major builder of street railway equipment, first producing horse and cable cars and later electric streetcar equipment from 1868 to 1941.

Vine Street and Albany Avenue are pictured in March 2005. The area is no longer agricultural and now has taxi service instead of trolley cars.

In this 1910 scene, car No. 626 is temporarily out of service, blocking Central Row, as it has "derailed." The wheels have gone two different directions, leaving the track and putting the car on the city street, a phenomenon described as "splitting a switch." Derailments like this were common when the cars ran on street track. The shop crew would have this back on the rails in no time. (Connecticut Electric Railway Association Archives.)

Car No. 3101 appears in this 1940 view with two unidentified operators. This was part of an order for 50 cars placed with the Osgood Bradley Company of Worcester, Massachusetts, in 1923. No. 3101 was later bought, along with others, by the Johnstown Traction Company of Johnstown, Pennsylvania, after the Hartford division converted to bus in 1941. Other cars in the 3100 series were sold to Vera Cruz, Mexico, where some ran until the 1970s. No. 3101 was scrapped sometime in the late 1940s.

In the 1920s, streets were not plowed; however, this did not deter trolley car service. This lightweight car, a more modern trolley car built entirely out of metal rather than the previous wood and metal combination, travels on Farmington Avenue at Mountain Road in West Hartford in the 1920s. No. 2314's operator is Caiss Anderson.

The first buses used in Hartford, as in other areas, were structured much like trolley cars. Built by the REO Motor Company in 1921, these early buses are pictured at the Vernon Street shops on August 25, 1921.

Car No. 1741 runs along Blue Hills Avenue at Mount St. Benedict Cemetery on September 11, 1935. Prior to 1932, this line continued on to Bloomfield Center.

The Isle-of-Safety was located on State Street in Hartford, as shown in this 1935 scene. This was the hub of streetcar operations in the Hartford area, with all lines either terminating or passing this site. When buses took over the routes, this remained a welcome shelter for downtown travelers. In 1990, the shelter was disassembled and moved to the Connecticut Trolley Museum in East Windsor, where it can be seen today.

The Isle-of-Safety is pictured at the Connecticut Trolley Museum in 2004.

In this 1907 scene of Main Street and Central Row, the Old State House serves as Hartford City Hall, and the post office and customs house appear in the background. City hall moved into a new building farther south on Main Street in 1911, and the post office building was razed in the 1930s. Motor vehicle laws in Connecticut had just come into effect in 1901; the maximum speed limit was 12 miles per hour. Connecticut was the first state in the country to place regulations on automobiles, requiring such things as licensing for both cars and drivers.

In this 1935 view of the waiting area of the Isle-of-Safety, car No. 1238 departs down Asylum Street.

This overhead view of the intersection at Main and Asylum Streets, taken on July 16, 1930, shows the track arrangement allowing cars to go in one of three directions after leaving the Isle-of-Safety platform. Note the Phoenix National Bank building on the left. The second bank to be chartered in Connecticut, it was founded by an Episcopal layman. The first building on this site, opposite the Old State House, served as the rostrum for Stephen Douglas in 1860, when he gave a speech while campaigning for the presidency against Abraham Lincoln. After many mergers, the Phoenix Bank is now part of Bank of America. (*Hartford Courant* photograph.)

In May 1928, the Wethersfield Avenue carbarn housed not only the streetcars but also the operational headquarters of the Hartford division of the Connecticut Company. This building still stands, now home to various commercial enterprises. (F. S. Bennett Collection.)

Track is under construction on Capen Street in this August 1938 photograph. Long sleeves and hats were the standard of the day, even in the heat of the summer. Most of the track gangs were still Irish or Italian, even as late as the 1930s.

As late as 1938, one could still see horse-drawn wagons on the city streets, as evidenced by this Capen Street construction scene. This vegetable wagon delivered its goods right to your kitchen door.

Streetcar companies were subject to a variety of taxes and franchise fees; they were required to clean and sprinkle streets, as well as remove snow on streets with their tracks. The companies were also billed by the city for their share of the paving done between the tracks. Here, snowplow No. 0211 appears on Main Street at Atheneum Square South in February 1934.

The Travelers Insurance Company tower in downtown Hartford changed the landscape of the city forever. Its construction is shown in this 1917 scene. The tower took 10 years to complete and was finally finished in 1919. Until the 1970s, it was the tallest building in New England.

A Wethersfield-bound car passes the small park at the South Green in Hartford. The South Green originally served as the circus ground for the city until a new, larger site became available on Barbour Street in the north end of the city. It was at Barbour Street that the fatal circus fire occurred in 1944.

Car No. 53, shown here at the Vernon Street car yard in 1934, was one of a number of Putnam division cars transferred to Hartford after the Putnam lines closed in 1925. Built in 1898 by the Wason Manufacturing Company, it was scrapped in Hartford in 1935 after nearly 40 years of service.

An unidentified operator poses on open car No. 347 on Jordan Lane in Wethersfield in 1910.

As more buses were obtained, they got bigger; however, they still maintained the trolley car body style. Bus No. 74, a 1924 Pierce-Arrow 29-passenger model, is shown here in the new motor coach garage on Washington Street in Hartford in 1930.

At the end of the trolley era in Hartford, many of the cars were sold or destroyed. Here, open car No. 1245 is being scrapped at Vernon Street in 1935. The car was former Farmington Street Railway No. 4.

This unidentified group poses with an early REO bus in Hartford in the 1920s. They are most likely Connecticut Company and Public Utility Commission officials.

As more and more lines were motorized, more and more trolley cars sat idle. The backyard of the Vernon Street carbarn is loaded with extra equipment in this 1938 photograph. By this time, the business decision had been made to motorize all the Hartford lines.

The streetcar companies converted their line maintenance vehicles to motorized units, such as this 1920s-era Mack line maintenance truck working on Zion Street in April 1937. These vehicles replaced the horse-drawn tower wagons used in the early days of the street railways. They would respond to emergency situations to repair accident damage to poles and overhead wire. They also responded to multiple-alarm fires on trolley routes because big fires always resulted in hoses crossing the tracks, requiring the laying down of hose jumpers to allow the cars to continue. The line crew would even take down some overhead wire to allow the aerial ladders and water towers to operate at the fire scene.

Parks were a popular destination for trolley cars. This view at the end of the Barbour Street line on Tower Avenue shows the entrance to Hartford's Keney Park.

74

For the longer runs, interurban cars were run, rather than trolley cars. Former Rockville line interurban car No. 951 turns from Main Street onto State Street in this 1939 view. The interurban line ran on the New Haven Railroad tracks from Burnside Avenue in East Hartford to Vernon and up the branch line to Rockville. This line was discontinued in September 1924, and the cars were transferred for use on the Hartford city lines.

Single-truck Birney cars were the primary equipment used to provide service on the Broad Street line, which was converted to motor coach service in August 1931.

This view, looking south on Main Street in 1925, shows the increase in number of automobiles and decrease in trolley cars. Every building in this scene has since been razed.

A Wethersfield-bound car travels on Albany Avenue at Baltimore Street in 1938.

Four

THE HARTFORD SUBURBAN LINES

The Hartford Street Railway had a carbarn on Main Street in East Hartford, just north of the New Haven Railroad crossing. This barn, used to store cars for the East Windsor Hill line, was torn down in 1914. Prior to 1907, passengers traveling north of the railroad crossing had to change cars, as the trolley tracks did not cross the New Haven Railroad main line for safety reasons. In 1907, a bridge was built to allow passengers to travel to East Windsor Hill and beyond without changing cars.

This view of the North End carbarn in East Hartford includes a Hartford Street Railway single-truck open car. This car and the others stored in this barn ran between the New Haven Railroad crossing on Main Street and East Windsor Hill.

Hartford-bound interurban cars traveling near Long Hill Road in East Hartford, as seen in this c. 1920 view, ran on the New Haven Railroad tracks and therefore utilized signaling, which was not commonly found on trolley lines in the Hartford area. From 1908 to 1924, the Connecticut Company operated the Rockville interurban line with five cars from East Hartford to Rockville on the New Haven Railroad. This rail line is still in operation, providing freight service to customers in Manchester.

Car No. 1214 sits at a stop on the line to Glastonbury in 1933 while running down Main Street in East Hartford, near the present-day Hockanum School. The Glastonbury line had a very severe accident in the fall of 1915, when an express car bound for Glastonbury collided head-on with a northbound passenger car that had forgotten to wait at Hales Siding. The passenger car motorman was instantly killed, and both cars suffered substantial damage.

Periodic maintenance was a necessity on the trolley lines. In this 1935 view of Burnside Avenue in East Hartford, the line crew, aided by an old truck, completes some pole work.

A Hartford and Springfield Street Railway car, inbound to Hartford from Springfield around 1910, travels down the line from East Windsor Hill. The Comstock Building, featured in this scene, still stands today. Hartford and Springfield Street Railway cars ran on Connecticut Company lines from East Windsor Hill through downtown Hartford to Windsor. Cars came down the east side of the river and returned to Springfield on the west side; other cars ran in reverse. Through service between Hartford and Springfield ended on the west side in 1925 and on the east side in 1926.

The Comstock Building, located on Burnside Avenue, is pictured in 2005. Streetcars last ran past this building in November 1939, when the Manchester line was converted to bus.

During the flood of March 1936, Connecticut Boulevard was flooded, stranding all the Glastonbury and Manchester streetcars and buses on the east side of the river, many of them waiting on Main Street in East Hartford.

This view, looking west from Church Corners, proves that traversing Connecticut Boulevard in March 1936 was quite difficult. The horse-drawn milk wagon is the only vehicle able to negotiate the floodwaters.

Hartford division portable substation car No. 0281 is shown in East Hartford in the 1930s. The car, built by the General Electric Company in 1912, was used to convert high-voltage AC into 600 volts DC for use by streetcars. It could be moved around the system as needed if one of the stationary substations was off-line.

The hurricane of September 1938 was particularly severe. Storm damage was found throughout the state. Even on Burnside Avenue in East Hartford, trees were down throughout the area. After the storm, the overhead wire on the Manchester line was replaced—unlike the Glastonbury line, which was converted to motor coach—only to have the line abandoned in November 1939.

With all the railroad companies and competition for track usage, trolley cars were occasionally hitting and being hit by railroad equipment. Connecticut Company No. 950 and Case Brothers Company locomotive No. 1 have collided in this 1920s scene on Burnside Avenue in East Hartford. Case Brothers had its own three-quarter-mile railroad that connected with the New Haven Railroad to ship paper goods from the mill and receive coal and other supplies. (*Hartford Courant* photograph.)

Case Brothers No. 1 appears at the mill in East Hartford with its regular engineer, Bill Jett, in 1915. No. 1 was built by the Baldwin Locomotive Works for the South Manchester Railroad in 1879. It ran on that line until about 1914, when it was purchased by Case Brothers, which operated it until its replacement by another South Manchester engine in 1935. Throughout No. 1's time at the mill, it was run by its African American engineer Bill Jett, who had a reputation for knowing more about steam locomotives than anyone else at the mill. Jett died on the job in the late 1930s at the age of 80.

Conversion to a work car prolonged the life of many single-truck passenger cars long after they were no longer useful to carry passengers. This car was built in 1905 by the J. G. Brill Company for the Meriden division of the Consolidated Railway as passenger car No. 98. In 1915, it became No. 810 and then No. 0364 in 1931, when it was converted to a rail grinder car. Rail grinders were used to smooth over rough track joints in the street. It is shown here on Burnside Avenue near Tolland Street in East Hartford on October 28, 1935.

In addition to passengers, streetcar companies also carried freight. The interurban line to Rockville had stopped carrying passengers in regular service in 1924, but the New Haven Railroad interchange was still used by the Connecticut Company to receive cars for freight customers in East Hartford and Glastonbury. Burnside yard was closed in 1957, when the trackage on Burnside Avenue was abandoned in favor of a new line connecting with the New Haven Railroad at the Main Street overpass. Burnside Junction in East Hartford is pictured in the 1920s.

Inbound to Hartford from Glastonbury, car No. 1213 crosses Main Street in East Hartford on March 22, 1937. The United Aircraft and Transport Company complex is visible in the background. This was the location of Pratt and Whitney Aircraft, Hamilton Standard Propeller, and Chance Vought divisions of the company, the predecessor of the United Technologies Corporation.

Express car No. 2023 travels southbound on Main Street in East Hartford, en route to the J. B. Williams Company in Glastonbury. As a subsidiary of the New Haven Railroad, the Connecticut Company was able to interchange freight cars with the main line railroads. Most railroads had poor relations with streetcar and interurban lines and refused to exchange freight or allow them to participate in freight service. Its relationship with the New Haven Railroad allowed the Connecticut Company to develop a sizeable amount of freight traffic on the Glastonbury line. The J. B. Williams Company regularly shipped carloads of toiletries to its warehouses in Los Angeles and San Francisco.

Sharing the roads with automobile traffic proved to be hazardous at times, as seen in this photograph of Connecticut Company diesel locomotive No. 0809 and a taxi cab involved in an accident on Main Street in East Hartford in March 1964. The East Hartford freight line was the last vestige of the vast Connecticut Company streetcar system in the Hartford area. After the Hartford lines were converted to an all-bus operation in 1941, the East Hartford–Glastonbury freight line continued to operate using former express cars converted to self-propelled locomotives. In 1957, the line operated using former New Haven Railroad General Electric 44-ton locomotives.

Hartford and Wethersfield Horse Railroad No. 99 is shown here. The line from East Hartford Center to Glastonbury was actually chartered by the East Hartford and Glastonbury Horse Railroad in 1866, although the company never actually built any lines. About 1886, the Hartford and Wethersfield Horse Railroad constructed the line from East Hartford to Glastonbury. In 1899, the name was changed to the East Hartford and Glastonbury Street Railway, with the Hartford Street Railway assuming all the stock.

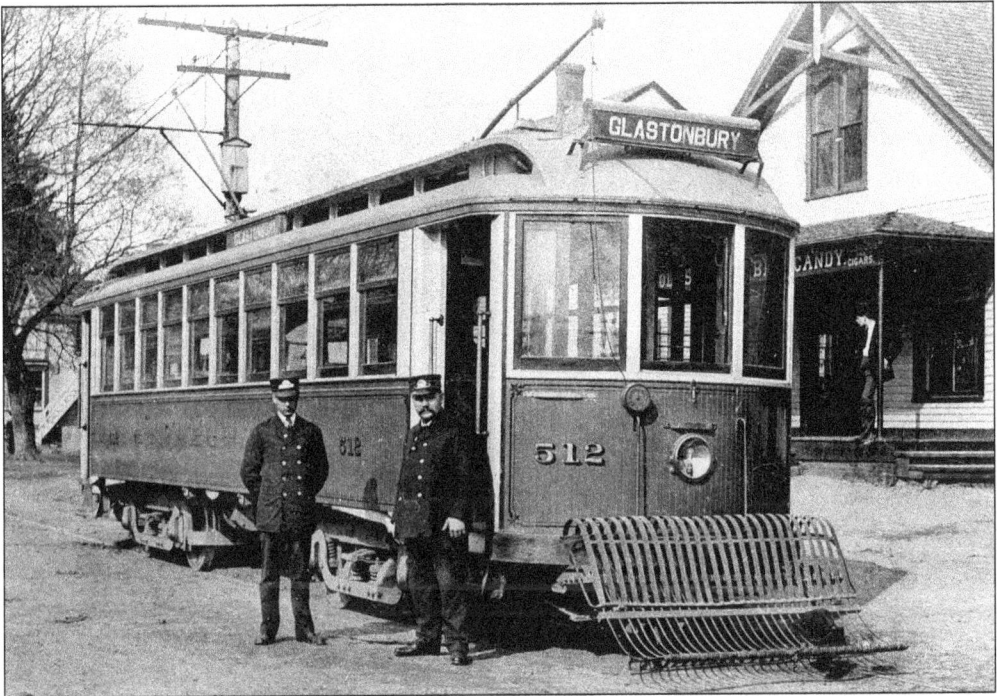

Connecticut Company car No. 512 sits at the end of the line on Water Street in South Glastonbury in 1909. In 1892, the line was opened from Church Corners in East Hartford to Hubbard Street in Glastonbury; the next year, it was extended to Roaring Brook in South Glastonbury. On June 17, 1928, the line from South Glastonbury was cut back to Hubbard Street due to paving by the state highway department. The light passenger volume did not make it economically feasible for the Connecticut Company to spend several hundred thousand dollars to include new tracks in the project.

Hartford Street Railway open car No. 126 appears at the end of the line in South Glastonbury in this 1895 scene. Many Hartford residents rode the open cars to Brookside Park, located at the end of the trolley line, in the summer months.

Express car No. 2023 is en route to the J. B. Williams plant on Hubbard Street in Glastonbury in March 1936. The line on Hubbard Street was built in 1908 to allow J. B. Williams to receive and ship via rail. The half-mile line was never used for regular passenger service. Another freight customer on the Glastonbury line was Hales Orchards, which shipped all over the country during the peach season in the early 1900s. The Hales were pioneers in the nationwide marketing of produce. This was made possible because of the freight service provided by the Hartford Street Railway and later the Connecticut Company.

MAIN STREET · SO. MANCHESTER, CONN.

Main Street in South Manchester is the subject of this early-1900s postcard view. The tracks were later moved to the center of the street. This line was converted to motor coach on November 5, 1939. (Steve Kellner Collection.)

This 1937 view depicts the same location as the previous image. The South Manchester line was leased from the Manchester Electric Company, formerly South Manchester Light Power and Tramway, for $600 per year. The .788-mile line ran from Manchester Center to the terminus at South Manchester. The Connecticut Company paid all maintenance, repairs, and taxes. The principal business of the Manchester Electric Company was selling electricity in Manchester for lighting and power. The company was controlled by the Cheney family, owners of the vast silk mill operations.

Many of the buildings remain in this 2005 view of Main Street in Manchester; however, the streetcars have now been gone from city streets for over 66 years.

The shop crew of the Hartford, Manchester and Rockville Tramway poses for a group photograph in 1897. From left to right are George House, Jack Gordon, Clarence Tracy, Tom Smithe, and Pat Fitzpatrick. (F. S. Bennett Collection.)

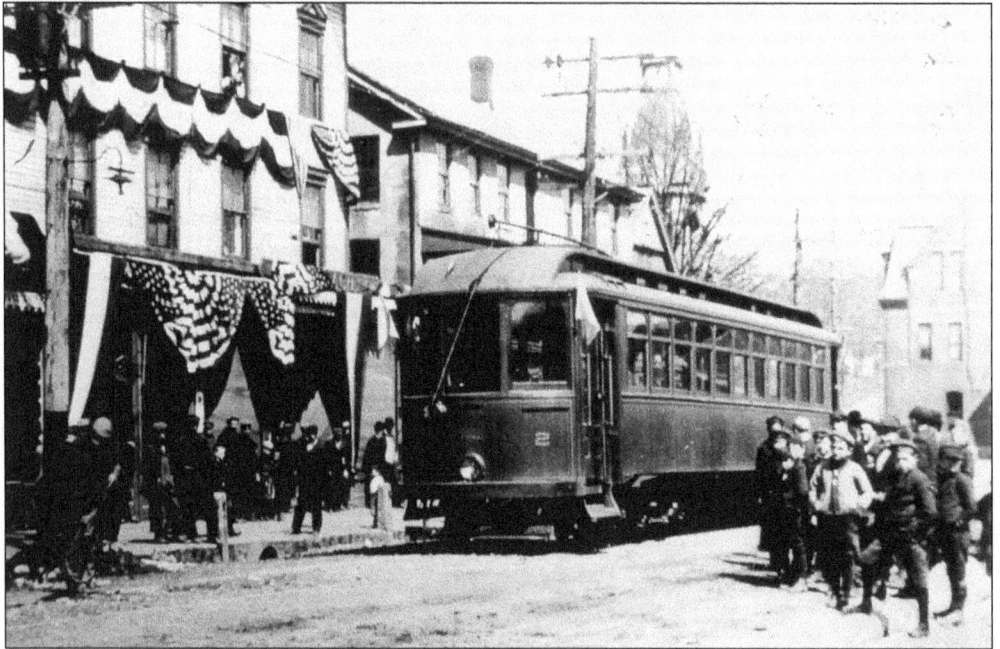

Local residents watch as Consolidated Railway car No. 2 passes through Stafford Springs, heading back to Hartford, on the first day of operation in April 20, 1908. (Connecticut Electric Railway Association Archives.)

The last run of the Rockville–Hartford interurban line was operated by car No. 1209 on September 28, 1924. Some of the same people who rode on the first trip in 1908 also made the last. The interurban line was scheduled for discontinuation in February 1917, and the New Haven Railroad planned a new train service to replace the streetcars, but popular opinion favored the retention of the interurban line, as it provided better service. After it was in fact discontinued in 1924, the New Haven Railroad scheduled a daily train running from Rockville to Union Station in Hartford in the morning and back in the evening. By 1931, that train was gone too, no doubt a victim of the automobile.

Hartford, Manchester and Rockville Tramway car No. 26 travels on Main Street in the Talcottville section of Vernon. The company started in 1894, building lines in East Hartford, Manchester, and Rockville. The line was purchased by the Consolidated Railway in 1906 and eventually became part of the Connecticut Company's Hartford division.

This view shows East Main Street in Rockville in the early 1900s. (Steve Kellner Collection.)

The New Britain line ran near the Balf Company quarry on Newington Avenue in Hartford, as seen here in 1899. This car was originally built with open platforms that afforded the motormen little protection in bad weather.

The railroad and streetcar companies seldom shared the same trackage. This New Britain car crosses the New Haven Railroad line at Maple Hill in Newington around 1910. The bridge was torn down in 1938 after the abandonment of the line in 1937.

This photograph, taken from the motorman's point of view on February 28, 1937, depicts the bridge over the New Haven Railroad in Newington on the New Britain line.

Following the transition from streetcar to motor coach, much of the trackage was removed, as shown in this April 1934 scene on Farmington Avenue at Sunset Terrace.

This August 1937 view shows Prospect Avenue near Capital Avenue. This area was included on the Elizabeth Park line, which originally ran all the way to St. Mary's Home on Steele Road in West Hartford. By 1937, the line only ran from Park Street to Farmington Avenue. Motor coach service replaced the streetcars in 1926, with buses traveling to the park via Asylum Avenue.

No. 1215 sits on Park Road at South Quaker Lane in West Hartford in 1938. It will soon leave for the Old State House in downtown Hartford. No. 1215 was a former Middletown division car that came to Hartford in 1925.

Shown here is a view of the above location in 2005.

The line came to an end at New Britain Avenue in the Elmwood section of West Hartford, seen in 1905. The Elmwood and Blue Hills Avenue lines were combined, with cars running between the two points via the Old State House in downtown Hartford.

Hartford Street Railway car No. 251 travels on New Britain Avenue in the Elmwood section of West Hartford. The New Haven Railroad main line appears in the background of this 1895 image.

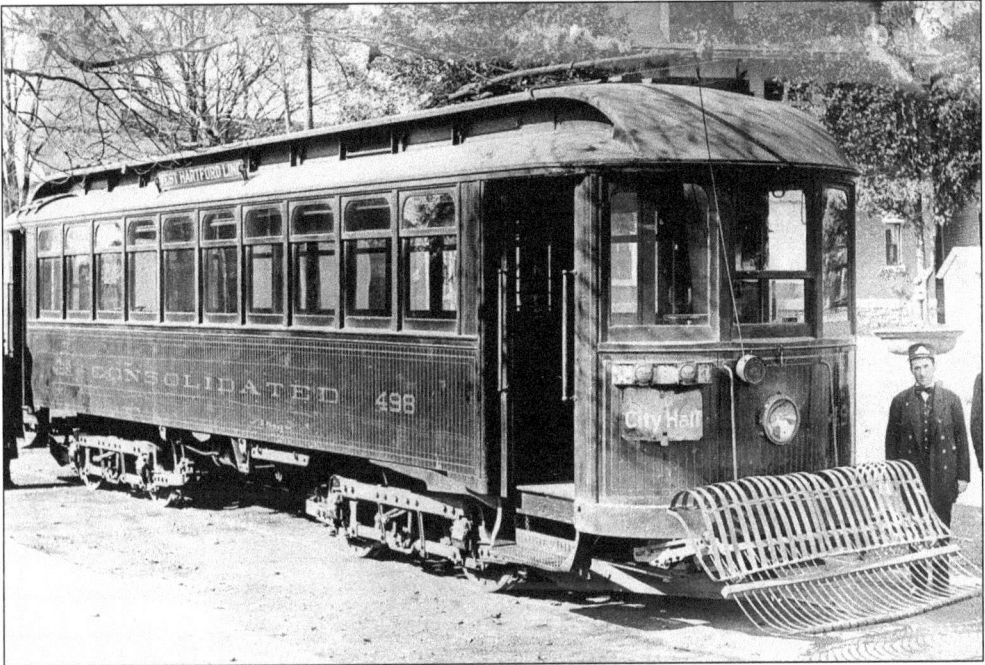

Consolidated Railway No. 498 waits to depart West Hartford Center for a run back to downtown Hartford in 1908. No. 498 was a product of the Wason Manufacturing Company of Springfield, Massachusetts, and operated in Hartford until being scrapped in 1937. Track from West Hartford Center to Unionville was owned and operated by the Farmington Street Railway. Its cars ran to downtown Hartford via the Consolidated Railway Farmington Avenue line to the Old State House. (F. S. Bennett Collection.)

Hartford Street Railway car No. 137 sits at the end of the Rainbow line in Windsor in this 1897 view. In October 1930, streetcar service from Windsor Center to Rainbow was converted to motor coach. The motor coach would run out to Windsor in the morning and shuttle passengers from Windsor Center to Rainbow all day, meeting all the streetcars outbound from Hartford. In the evening, it would return to the Vernon Street carbarn for the night.

Many streetcar lines transported people from the city to the country on the weekends. This car appears at Rainbow Park in the Poquonock section of Windsor on June 23, 1897. A note on the back of the photograph indicates that this was the first trolley excursion for these people from Newington.

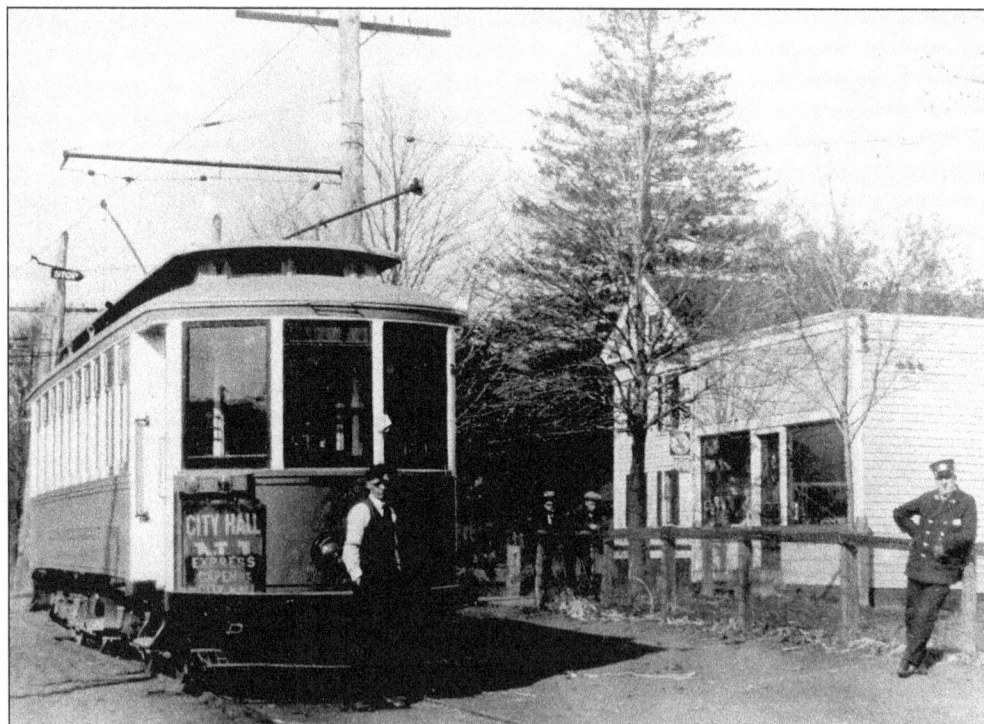

This scene occurred at the end of the line in the Rainbow section of Windsor about 1918. The building still stands today, although greatly modified.

Car No. 1936 runs on the Windsor line in this 1936 view.

Car No. 1163 sits at the end of the line in Windsor Center on February 17, 1940.

Former Putnam division car No. 65 operated on the Windsor line in 1940. It came to Hartford in 1925, after the Putnam lines closed down. After streetcars were discontinued in 1941, this car was acquired by the Connecticut Trolley Museum in East Windsor.

Prior to the advent and common usage of the two-way radio, many streetcar companies used telephones to communicate with the motormen. Dispatching on the Hartford lines was exclusively done by telephone. The dispatcher was in direct contact with the motormen and conductors, trusting the men to interpret and remember the verbal instructions properly. The Connecticut Company maintained an extensive telephone system on its lines with phones located at all important junctions and passing sidings.

Five

NEW BRITAIN, PLAINVILLE, AND SOUTHINGTON

Lake Compounce in Bristol was served by both the Connecticut Company and the Bristol Traction Company, although there was no physical connection between the lines. Car No. 503 rests at Lake Compounce, waiting to return to Lazy Lane in Southington, where it will connect with cars running on the Plainville–New Haven line.

Two Connecticut Company cars meet in downtown Plainville in this 1920 postcard view. According to the caption on the card, one was a double-truck closed car and the other a semi-convertible car.

This photograph provides an early view of mass transit in New Britain in 1898. The Central Railway and Electric Company would soon become part of the vast Connecticut Railway and Lighting Company. This car still has an open vestibule, exposing the motorman to all types of weather. Most cars of this era had little or no heat, so the passengers inside the car would not have been much warmer than the motorman.

A number of small street railway companies operated throughout Connecticut, meaning that two different companies could serve the same town. This 1898 view of Plainville shows a flurry of activity as cars from New Britain, served by the Connecticut Railway and Lighting Company, and Meriden, served by the Meriden, Southington, and Compounce Tramway Company, meet downtown.

The Chestnut Street carbarn in New Britain is pictured in this 1918 scene. After New Britain streetcar service was discontinued in 1937, this building served as a bus garage until the 1960s.

Single-truck open car No. 69 lays over in downtown New Britain in 1915. Due to the advances in technology, cars like this would only run for a few more years; made in the mid-1890s, they were already obsolete. Newer cars were bigger, smoother, and more economical to run, as they were designed to be one-man operations.

A jam-packed open car of Connecticut Company predecessor Central Railway and Electric appears at the Berlin railroad station in 1896. No. 65 ran until 1920, when it was finally scrapped.

104

Double-truck wood passenger car No. 1522 is shown in Plainville in 1935. Passengers for Bristol had to walk across the railroad, shown in the background, to board a Bristol Traction Company car, as the Bristol system was not physically connected to the Connecticut Company system.

In this 1919 view of Central Square, New Britain, the car to the left is one of the 1822-1831-series interurban cars built in 1918 for service on the Hartford–New Britain line. These cars were scrapped after the abandonment of service in 1937.

A 1500-series car operates on the New Britain–Plainville line in 1935. Though it could use a coat of paint, streetcar service would soon end, and the Connecticut Railway Lighting Company had no plans to improve any cars.

Connecticut Company car No. 503, shown on February 21, 1921, lost brakes on Southington Mountain, derailed, and was almost cut in half by a large maple tree. The car was scrapped on the spot within a few days.

Six

THE HARTFORD AND SPRINGFIELD STREET RAILWAY

An Enfield and Longmeadow Electric Railway open car travels on Depot Street in the Warehouse Point section of East Windsor in this early view. Note the New Haven Railroad bridge over the Connecticut River through the highway bridge.

Enfield and Longmeadow Electric Railway car No. 4 runs on Main Street in the Warehouse Point section of East Windsor in this 1897 view, looking north from Bridge Street. The company started in 1896 with a route from Thompsonville to the state line to connect with streetcars from Springfield. The line was extended to Warehouse Point in 1897. In 1901, the company was reorganized as the Hartford and Springfield Street Railway with charters to build additional lines in central Connecticut. Car No. 4 was built by the J. G. Brill Company in 1896. It was later sold to the Hartford, Manchester and Rockville Tramway, where it became No. 48. The tramway merged with the Connecticut Company, and No. 48 became No. 684, running in Middletown until being scrapped in 1929.

In this March 2005 view of Main Street in Warehouse Point, note that the house in the middle of the 1897 photograph still stands.

Hartford and Springfield Street Railway car No. 14 appears at the corner of Main and Bridge Streets in Warehouse Point in 1910.

A Springfield Street Railway car, with a Hartford and Springfield crew, is shown in the Hazardville section of Enfield. The Hartford and Springfield Street Railway regularly borrowed cars from the Connecticut Company and the Springfield Street Railway. On a few occasions, the company even used equipment from the Holyoke Street Railway.

In 1908, Hartford and Springfield Street Railway car No. 15 sits at the end of the Rockville line on Bridge Street in Warehouse Point. The building behind the car still stands. The line to Rockville was built between 1905 and 1906. The company maintained its headquarters, car shop, and power plant in Warehouse Point from 1901 until the line closed in 1926. During its entire history, the firm remained independent and somehow avoided being acquired by the Connecticut Company, which operated over 90 percent of the street railway track in Connecticut.

The Thompsonville carbarn, pictured about 1900, was located near the present Enfield Town Hall. In addition to this barn, the line had a small facility in Windsor Locks, with the main carbarn located in Warehouse Point.

The first official trip into Rockville by the Hartford and Springfield Street Railway occurred in 1906. Car No. 31 is shown at Park Square. (Steve Kellner Collection.)

Car No. 33 of the Hartford and Springfield Street Railway travels on Central Row by the old post office building in Hartford. Standing in front of the Old State House, the building was razed in the 1930s.

Car No. 25 was originally ordered from the Wason Manufacturing Company in 1905 by the Rockville, Broad Brook, and East Windsor Street Railway. By the time it was delivered in 1906, the line had been acquired by the Hartford and Springfield Street Railway.

This Thompsonville scene reveals the trolley waiting station on the right. The Enfield and Longmeadow Electric Railway originally built this line from the Connecticut state line to Thompsonville in 1896.

Thanksgiving Day 1905 offered this view of the Scantic River trestle on the Rockville line, just west of Broad Brook Center. The line was completed to Rockville in 1906.

This view of Ellington Center on April 7, 1917, shows the funeral of John Thompson. The car in the scene does not have an overhead destination sign on the front, so we know that it is not a Hartford and Springfield Street Railway car; it most likely came from Hartford or Springfield with the casket and mourners. While some of the street railways had cars specifically equipped for funerals, this was not the case with the Hartford and Springfield Street Railway. The company had trackage rights from the Connecticut Company to operate its cars directly into Hartford and Rockville and had the same arrangement with the Springfield Street Railway to operate into Springfield.

The Thompsonville waiting station is pictured in 1918. The motorman is identified as Francis Lefebvre of Windsor. After the Hartford and Springfield line quit in 1926, he became a chauffeur for the Chamberlain family. Lefebvre was also an operator at the Connecticut Trolley Museum from 1955 until the late 1970s.

Looking west, this 1918 view of Main Street in Somersville shows the end of the Thompsonville line. After the line was closed in 1926, bus service was provided on a limited schedule; by 1930, this service was gone and the area has not had public transportation since.

This Enfield and Longmeadow Electric Railway construction crew, on Enfield Street in Thompsonville in 1896, looks ready to perform any repairs or maintenance needed on the line. Car No. 1, seen here, is actually a snowplow with the blades removed for the summer. Due to the limited finances of many of the streetcar companies, equipment was used for more than one purpose.

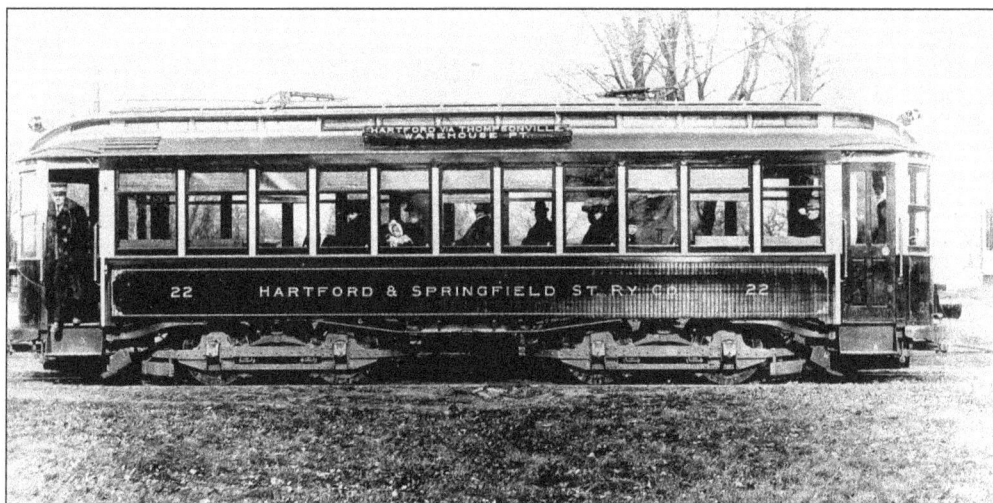

Railway companies acquired streetcars from many different small car manufacturers. Car No. 22 was built by the Laconia Car Company of Laconia, New Hampshire, in 1902. After the line closed in 1926, most of the cars were taken to Piney Ridge Park on the Rockville line and burned for the metal in the bodies. In 1924, four open cars were sold to the New Haven and Shore Line Railway for use on its line to Hammonasset Park.

The Hartford and Springfield Street Railway crossed the Armory branch of the New Haven Railroad in Melrose on this trestle. The white building on the left is now the Melrose Library.

A Hartford and Springfield Street Railway car crosses under the New Haven Railroad Springfield line in Windsor Center, heading north to Windsor Locks and Springfield, in this 1914 view. In 1915, a new bridge was built to eliminate the hazardous situation that existed. It was one of the first highway underpass replacement projects in the state of Connecticut. (Connecticut Electric Railway Association Archives.)

TROLLEY WRECK AT SCITICO, DEC. 10, 1904.

Car No. 22 was en route to Somersville at 6:30 a.m. on December 10, 1904, when it lost brakes on the long hill between Hazardville and Scitico, crashing into a house next to the road. The car smashed into the front parlor, doing extensive damage. Two children were sleeping on the second floor over where the car entered the house. No one was hurt, although the company had a rather large claim for property damage. The house stood until the 1970s.

This photograph of Main Street in the East Windsor Hill section of South Windsor was taken in 1906. Here, the Connecticut Company line from Hartford ended and the Hartford and Springfield Street Railway line to Thompsonville and Springfield began. (Connecticut Electric Railway Association Archives.)

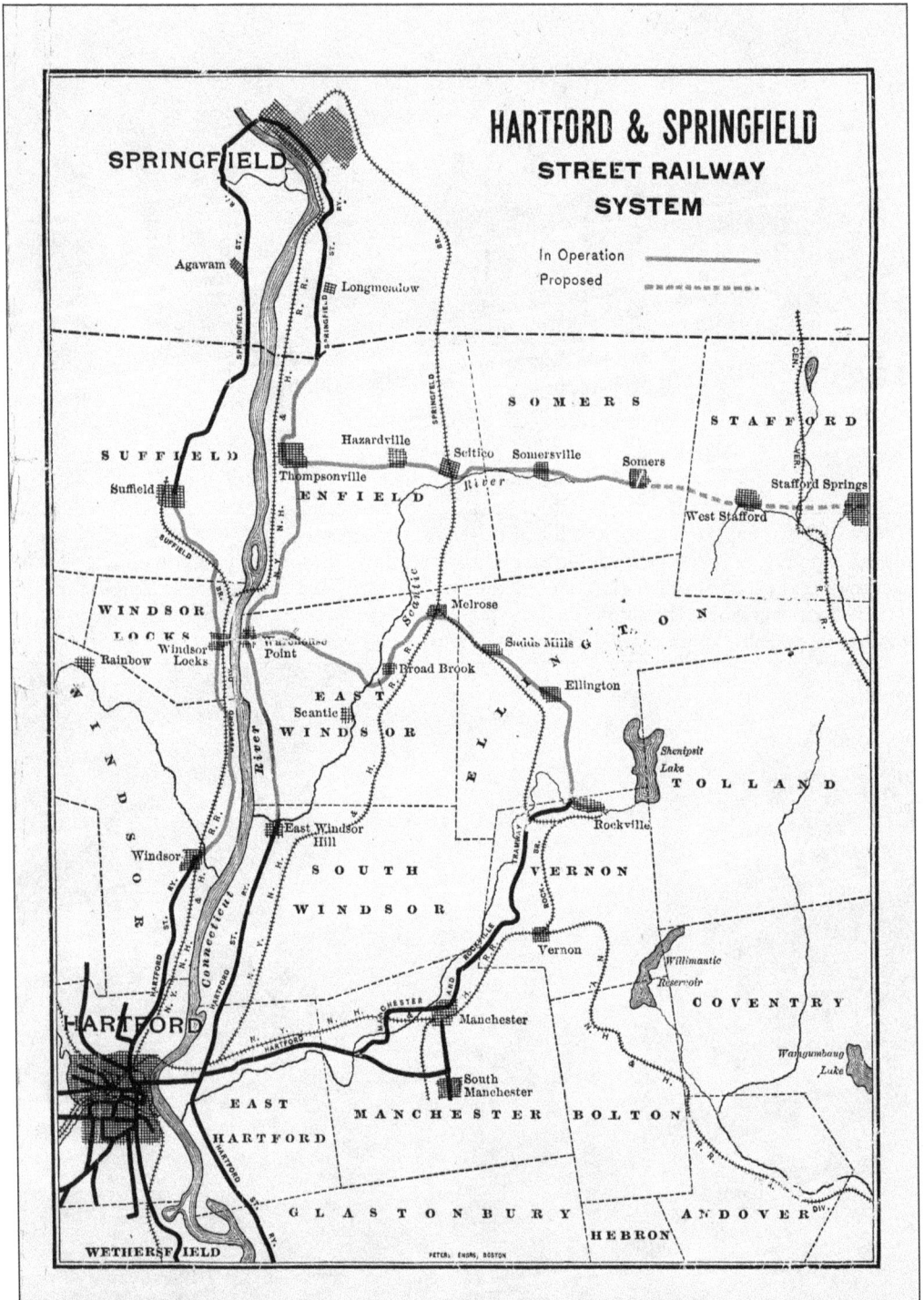

This map of the Hartford and Springfield Street Railway shows its connections to the Connecticut Company and the Springfield Street Railway. (F. S. Bennett Collection.)

Seven

THE CONNECTICUT TROLLEY MUSEUM IN 2005

Former Fairhaven and Westville Railroad Company open car No. 355, shown here in 1980, was built by the J. G. Brill Company in 1900. After the firm was absorbed into the Connecticut Company, the car was renumbered 663. It ran in New Haven until 1948, after which it was acquired by the Connecticut Trolley Museum. During the 1950s and 1960s, this car was carefully restored to what it looked like in 1900 by well-known streetcar restorer Fred Bennett. No. 355 still takes occasional trips on the old Hartford and Springfield line operated by the Connecticut Trolley Museum. The operator pictured is Kenneth DeCelle of Springfield, Massachusetts, who was a longtime volunteer at the museum. (Connecticut Electric Railway Association Archives.)

Part of the Rockville branch of the Hartford and Springfield Street Railway is still in use today. A three-and-one-half-mile section of the private right-of-way on the Rockville branch was purchased by the Connecticut Trolley Museum in 1940. This view looks east from North Road, about one mile from Warehouse Point.

Connecticut Company open car No. 840 is eastbound on the former Hartford and Springfield Rockville line in the 1960s. About a mile east of this location, the Hartford and Springfield Street Railway owned a recreational area called Piney Ridge Park. The facilities included a pavilion used for band concerts and dancing. A large baseball field was also located on the property and was used for minor-league games on Sundays, because Hartford had a city ordinance that prohibited ball playing on Sundays prior to 1914. The park was a major revenue contributor to the company in the summer months.

The old Hartford and Springfield line was the location of a test program conducted in the late 1960s by the Connecticut Company. The firm had proposed a regional transit system for passenger service provided by city transit buses modified to operate on the existing rail lines or the highways. Only one bus was outfitted with this equipment, No. 1712, which was a 1967 General Motors 53-passenger transit coach. The unique piece of rail equipment is now part of the collection at the Connecticut Trolley Museum.

No. 65 is shown in this August 1937 view on the Zion Street line; it was transported to the Connecticut Trolley Museum in 1941. (Connecticut Electric Railway Association Archives.)

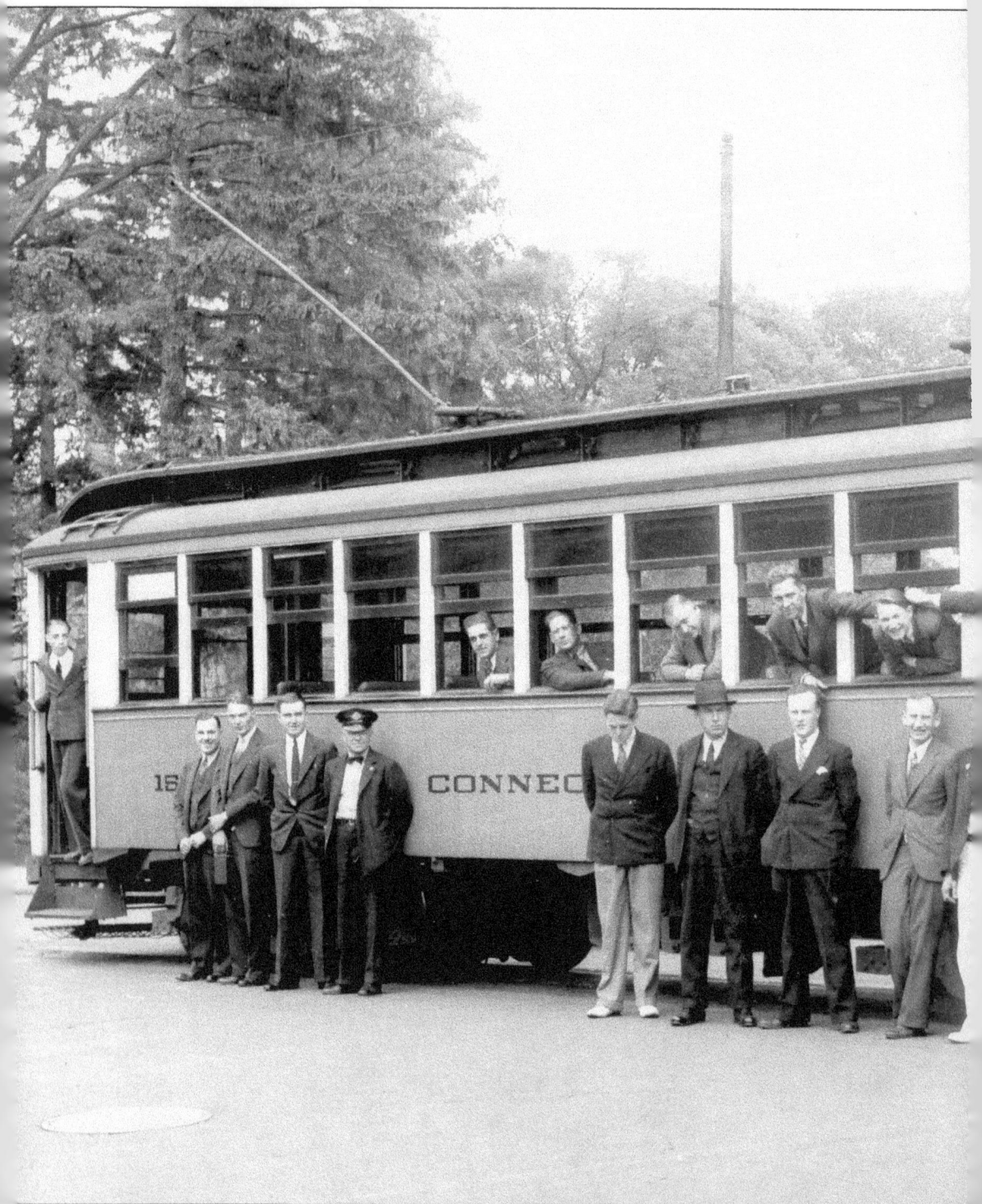

A car on Main Street at Hartford Road runs for trolley fans on the South Manchester line on June 5, 1938. No. 1565 was not normally used on the South Manchester line; 1900-series cars were used almost exclusively from the 1920s until the line was converted to bus in November 1939.

In this view are the three founding members of the Connecticut Electric Railway Association of the Connecticut Trolley Museum: Richard Whittier (far right), Henry Steig (third from right), and Roger Borrup (kneeling, eighth from right). (Connecticut Electric Railway Association Archives.)

New Orleans Public Service car No. 836 sits at North Road Station in East Windsor in this 1980s photograph, along with some volunteer operators. At this point, the Hartford and Springfield tracks left the public highway and ran over a private right-of-way for about four miles to the village of Broad Brook. This car, built in 1922 by the Perley Thomas Car Company of High Point, North Carolina, came to the Connecticut Trolley Museum in 1965. (Connecticut Electric Railway Association Archives.)

At a 1968 event of the National Railroad Association, two unique pieces of rail equipment meet at Hancock Siding on the Connecticut Trolley Museum line: Montreal Transport observation car No. 4, constructed in 1926, and Connecticut Company rail bus No. 1712, constructed by General Motors in 1967. No. 4 was built by the Montreal Street Railway's Hochelaga Shops, the last of four the company constructed. Such specially constructed sightseeing cars were especially popular in Canada, where similar equipment operated in Quebec, Calgary, and Vancouver. (William E. Wood photograph.)

In 1965, the Connecticut Trolley Museum purchased three open cars from Rio de Janeiro after the city's streetcar system was converted to motor coach. The three cars, along with nine others destined for other trolley museums, arrived in New York and, after being unloaded, were trucked the 125 miles to the museum in East Windsor. This photograph illustrates how all the equipment at the museum arrived; without a track connection to the national rail system, highway transportation is the only method available. (Connecticut Electric Railway Association Archives.)

Rio open car No. 1850 is lowered onto its wheels shortly after arriving at the Connecticut Trolley Museum in 1965. As the Rio de Janeiro lines were built to 4-foot-10-inch gauge, the trucks had to be modified to 4 feet 8½ inches before the car could operate at the museum. The Rio de Janeiro shops built hundreds of these cars around 1912 by copying an open car received in 1912 from the St. Louis Car Company. (Connecticut Electric Railway Association Archives.)

Since starting streetcar operations in 1955, the Connecticut Trolley Museum has hosted thousands of school field trips. The museum has provided a unique learning experience for children and adults alike. About 30 other streetcar museums operate in the United States and Canada, and today there are more trolley museums than trolley operators in North America. (Connecticut Electric Railway Association Archives.)

This nighttime view of a four-car lineup at the Connecticut Trolley Museum depicts, from left to right, No. 3333 (Boston, Massachusetts), No. 3001 (Torrington, Connecticut), No. 2600 (Montreal, Quebec), and No. 451 (St. Louis, Missouri). (Connecticut Electric Railway Association Archives.)

Both Connecticut car No. 840 and Rio car No. 1850 are Narragensett-type open cars, each of which can hold over 80 passengers. These large reliable cars were common on New England streetcar systems. (Connecticut Electric Railway Association Archives.)

When the Hartford and Springfield Street Railway lines were built in the early 1900s, they used lightweight rail, untreated wood ties, and dirt ballast. Manual labor was plentiful and relatively cheap at the time. The right-of-way grading was accomplished with dump carts pulled by horses or mules, wheelbarrows, picks, and shovels. After the Hartford and Springfield Street Railway went out of business in 1926, the track was removed. When purchasing the three-and-one-half-mile line in 1940, the Connecticut Electric Railway Association began to rebuild it with heavyweight rail, treated ties, and stone ballast. In this 1995 view, an eastbound train passes Woods carbarn, about 1,500 feet east of North Road Station. The demonstration signal system is visible in this view; needless to say, the old Hartford and Springfield never had the luxury of such an elaborate signaling system. (Connecticut Electric Railway Association Archives.)

www.ingramcontent.com/pod-product-compliance
Lightning Source LLC
Chambersburg PA
CBHW050631110426
42813CB00007B/1774